*a gift for*

_____

*from*

_____

*May you continue to grow
in love, wisdom, and joy
in your family.*

# 50
# ways
## to really
## love your
# kids

## Dr. Tim Kimmel

THOMAS NELSON
*Since 1798*

NASHVILLE   DALLAS   MEXICO CITY   RIO DE JANEIRO

Published in Nashville, Tennessee, by Thomas Nelson. Thomas Nelson is a registered trademark of Thomas Nelson, Inc.

*The New King James Version* (NKJV) ©1979, 1980, 1982, 1992, Thomas Nelson, Inc., Publisher. Used by permission.
*New Century Version*® (NCV). Copyright © 1987, 1988, 1991 by Thomas Nelson, Inc. All rights reserved. Used by permission.
*The King James Version* of the Bible (KJV).
*The New International Version of the Bible* (NIV) © 1984 by the International Bible Society. Used by permission of Zondervan Bible Publishers.

Design: The DesignWorks Group; cover, David Uttley; interior, Robin Black
www.thedesignworksgroup.com

Project Editor: Kathy Baker

ISBN 978-1-4041-0325-2

*Printed and bound in China*
10 11 12 13 14  WA  9 8 7 6 5 4 3 2

www.timkimmel.com | www.familymatters.net

*"Whoever receives one of these little children
in My name receives Me;
and whoever receives Me, receives not Me
but Him who sent Me."*

MARK 9:37 NKJV

# GIVE YOUR KIDS . . .

# Introduction

New things just keep coming up with kids.
> New clothes, new fads, new toys, new friends,
> new distractions.

> New health guidelines, new school standards,
> new driver's license requirements.

> New joys, new heartaches, new victories, new setbacks.

> New hopes, new questions.

Because we love our kids—*really* love them—we're
always on the lookout for new ways to make their precious
lives even better.

So how about finding new ways to love them? That's
where this little book can make a big difference. Here are
fifty practical ways (plus a bonus one thrown in for good
measure) that can sharpen your ability to bring the best out
of your children. Because you obviously love your kids,

you're no doubt already doing a lot of these recommendations. Good for you! But love is one of those dimensions in life that can always grow to new and more effective levels. And like all parents want to do a good job of loving their kids, you're not satisfied to let your love remain limited, stunted, or static. Thus: *50 Ways to Really Love Your Kids.* Many of these recommendations probably have never crossed your mind before, but you desperately need to consider them as you put the finishing touches on your son or daughter's childhood. By the time you finish the last vignette in this book you are going to have the insight needed to raise kids who grow up to be great adults. Let me encourage you to give them all a try.

> My child, listen to
> your father's teaching
> and do not forget
> your mother's advice.
>
> PROVERBS 1:8 NCV

Parenting is a sacred trust. You have been given an opportunity to teach your children how to live large and love deeply. Let these fifty-one ways help you set examples that will inspire and encourage your kids to a better and more satisfying future . . . all the way to forever.

# 1

## Love that is Secure

When did you first fall in love with your child? For some moms, it was about ten seconds after they saw the two lines on their home pregnancy test. For sure, the earliest movement from the miracle growing inside of them drew an echo of "I love you" from somewhere in the corners of their hearts. Dads sometimes take a bit longer to make the connection. But for certain, when we look into the eyes of that little life placed in our arms, the deal is sealed. We are in love.

It's safe to say that almost all parents love their children. But loving your child—and even doing things to show your love—does not necessarily translate into a secure love.

Secure love? What's that?

I'm talking about that steady, sure, and unwavering love that we must not fail to write on the hard drives of our children's souls. It's a complete love that they can default to when their hearts are under attack. It's the kind of love that children can confidently carry with them into the future.

Secure love is the stuff that helps them continue moving forward when they just got sucker punched by circumstances. Like when they've given their hearts to someone who has just told them they don't love them anymore, or the bottom falls out of their financial world, or they get fired, or framed, or betrayed. It's the love that keeps them confident when they're wearing a uniform, standing a lonely post, and facing a merciless enemy far from the safety of home.

I've got great news! You can set the foundation for this secure love. All you need to do is go to the source of a love that knows no boundaries and has no limits. A God who would cross the threshold of time, walk down a back street of civilization, and climb up on a cross that was meant for us knows how to help us love like that. And the better news is that He offers that love to anyone who asks for it.

Adapted from *Grace-Based Parenting* and *Little House on the Freeway*

## GIVE YOUR KIDS
# Love Without Conditions

Here's a problem: standard off–the–rack love comes with too many strings attached. Few things block our ability to connect to the hearts of our children more than a love that says, "I'll love you if, or . . . because, or . . . when, or . . . after certain *arbitrary* conditions have been met." That kind of love makes it hard for kids to keep a smile on their face, a gleam in their eye, or a bounce in their step.

Our children need an "I love you . . . period" kind of love, and they need it most from the people they care about most—Mom and Dad. They need to know that improvement on their part isn't going to get us to love them more, and that we won't love them any less if they have a bad day, or even a series of them.

This is where a well–defined love comes to the rescue. When we start with an unencumbered understanding of what unconditional love looks like, it's easier—a lot easier— to make it part of the DNA of our role as parents.

I've got a definition of love that you can take to the bank! This stuff works! Love is: *the commitment of my will to your needs and best interests, regardless of the cost.* Run it through the wringer. Take it through its paces. This kind of love passes the litmus test of unconditional love.

But it doesn't come cheap. You may have to muster courage, say "no" to your fears, and place your feelings in check. That's because unconditional love isn't about you; it's about *them*.

Unconditional love understands that loving your children is often inconvenient and painful. It will cost you money, time, and years of sleep. It might cost Mom decades off her career and too many years off her figure. It might cost Dad a promotion. You will have to do without some amenities or lavish vacations. It definitely means eating crow, swallowing your pride, and asking for forgiveness . . . a lot. But in your wallet are pictures of some kids who God says are definitely worth it.

Adapted from *Grace-Based Parenting*

## 3

## Give Your Kids

# Love that Provides
## a Place to Repent

The nature of a child's spirit begs a tender touch, whether it's emotions lost in confusion and badgered by fears, or a broken heart that longs to recover in the deep, quilted comfort of gentle understanding. Children lose their way. Sometimes they make huge mistakes in the process. They need a place to repent.

As adults, we know that those who follow the well–worn path to the base of the cross find ample room for heavy hearts and hurts that can't seem to heal. It's an amazing grace that doesn't trivialize the fickle nature of our personalities. There's no condescension waiting to counter our tendencies to become easily embarrassed. There are no lectures to straighten out the folly of our thinking. There's no mocking of our self–conscious thoughts—just a generous Savior with a gentle heart who knows how unsure we often are about ourselves.

God doesn't "card" those who come searching for His grace. You won't find any age restrictions for those wanting to travel down His path. Jesus said, "Let the little children come to me" (Matthew 19:4 NKJV). But some paths are easier to take when they are walked hand in hand with someone older and wiser.

Jesus makes people feel comfortable even when He catches them without their makeup. When circumstances scrub off the layers of their self–confidence and their shortcomings wash away the foundation of their self–righteousness, Jesus isn't appalled by the blemishes He finds underneath. There's no sin too bad, no doubt too big, no question too hard, and no heart too broken that His grace can't deal with it.

These are the very things that children need to learn early in their lives, and God has given parents the responsibility to be the gatekeepers of His grace. Your careful responses to these fragile issues play the key role in whether your children will even be inclined to head down the path to God's grace. Furthermore, your regular trips down this path for your own personal vulnerabilities make it easier for your children to trust you when you try to take their hands and show them the way.

Adapted from *Grace-Based Parenting*

## 4

### GIVE YOUR KIDS

# Love Saturated With Grace

If there is any single thing we can do that gives our children an overwhelming sense of being loved, it is to treat them the way God treats us. God deals with us according to His grace. I like to call this, "grace–based parenting."

Why *grace*?

Of all the qualifiers we could choose to describe the kind of parenting we are to do, why choose this one?

After all, the list of qualifiers is endless. Several that come to mind make a nice first impression: bold parenting, smart parenting, savvy parenting, tough parenting. But these fall short. They don't capture God's heart. They don't even come close. They only reflect our hearts, and as such they don't do that very well. Among other things, these styles of parenting are far too confining and a little too *inviting*.

Only one phrase covers all the bases—*grace–based parenting.* It captures the heart of God in an all–encompassing way. Grace includes His love, embraces His mercy, and honors His sacrifice.

You have been singled out to do a favor for God. He is asking you to be His representative to a small but vital part of the next generation. He needs someone to be His voice, His arms, and His heart. He chose you.

He chose you to assist Him in a miracle. He gave you children and then said, "Now go and give these precious lives *meaning*." You ask, "How on earth can I do that?"

The answer isn't on earth. It's found in heaven. It's sitting on an eternal throne. He has many names, but among one of the sweetest is "The God of Grace." So when you wonder, *How am I to raise up children to love and serve God?* The answer is actually not that difficult . . . all you need to do is treat your children the way God treats you.

He does it in His grace.

And here's the good part. If the only thing you get right as parents is His grace, everything else will be just fine.

Adapted from *Grace-Based Parenting*

## GIVE YOUR KIDS

# Love That is Quick to Forgive

It's second nature for our kids to let us down. Without trying hard, they can push every button designed to bring out the worst in us. If we were scorekeepers, it would be easy to wonder if this whole parenting gig is even worth it. It also would be easy to become bitter.

Ah, but bitterness is worse than death itself. It's a cancer that slowly works its way into the core of our character. Few things steal joy more than a parent who carries a grudge.

That's why we must set the standard of absolute forgiveness. And that's where the rub occurs. As much as we'd like to, many of us find the corridors of our hearts haunted by ghosts from the past. Walking corpses. Grotesque, bitter spirits that moan and linger and rattle their chains . . . because we have refused to forgive people who have done us wrong. We try and try, but it's so hard to pull ourselves from its shackles.

God's got the key.

He wants to turn the tumblers in the locks that keep us fettered. He wants to bring us out of the dungeons and into the light. It's hard though. It takes courage. Maybe that's why most people would rather rearrange the chips on their shoulders than refuse to put them there in the first place. Maybe that's why we keep sipping from that cheap whisky called revenge. It numbs our conscience and blurs our ability to see the truth.

When the crimes against my heart seem unforgivable, I am compelled to walk up a certain hill. It's the Hill of Forgiveness that sits at the center of civilization. The ground at the top is level. The grass growing at the base of the wooden stanchions ripples in the fresh breeze of freedom. There's always room for anyone wanting help for their hurts. And moms and dads who make regular trips to the top of this hill to claim its power give their children one of the greatest gifts a child needs to succeed—a living example of a heart that is always quick to forgive. Our kids will find it much easier to give what they have consistently received.

Adapted from *Homegrown Heroes* and *Little House on the Freeway*

# Love Known for Its Tender Touch

Allow me to let you in on a secret: God has hardwired our children's skins to their souls. As a result, He's made meaningful touch one of the greatest tools for transferring a sense of secure love to their hearts. The hugs and kisses they receive from both their mother and father create a reservoir of love in their hearts that can carry them through some of the worst moments life can dish up.

Sure, they get too big to hold on your lap. And they might become self-conscious about receiving affection in front of their friends. Some might even go through a stage where they turn away. But they still need meaningful touch, and deep down in their hearts, they *want* it.

A gifted classical musician comes to mind. The late Andor Foldes recalls how praise and a tender touch made all the difference for him early in his career. He was sixteen and already a skilled pianist. But he was at an all-time low because of a conflict with his piano teacher. During this time, however, one of the most renowned pianists of his day came to the city to perform. Emil von Sauer was not only famous because of his abilities at the piano but he also could claim the notoriety of being the last surviving pupil of Franz Liszt.

Sauer requested that Foldes play for him. Foldes obliged with some of the most difficult works of Bach, Beethoven, and Schumann. When he finished, Sauer walked over to him and kissed him on the forehead.

"My son," he said, "When I was your age I became a student of Liszt. He kissed me on the forehead after my first lesson, saying, 'Take good care of this kiss—it comes from Beethoven, who gave it to me after hearing me play.' I have waited for years to pass on this sacred heritage, but now I feel you deserve it."

Like Foldes's kiss from Beethoven, our children will be empowered through the challenges of childhood and sustained through the dark corridors of their future by the reserves of affection they've built up from our tender touch.

Adapted from *Little House on the Freeway*

# 7

## Love Backed up by Integrity

When I shipped off to seminary, meandered through the ivory towers of theology, and finally graduated into ministry, I was naive about a lot of things. For one, I had no idea how intensely I would be scrutinized.

It didn't take long before I realized that the people to whom I ministered held up a different yardstick to their own character than the one they held up to mine. That's because the ministry is a *character profession*. It's one of those livelihoods that demands that you practice what you preach. You can be an excellent plumber even though you cheat on your wife. You can be a sought–after attorney even though you get soused every night. But try to juggle those vices while standing behind the pulpit, and you will soon find yourself looking for a new platform.

Guess what?

*Parenting is a character profession!*

Children—who sleep in our back bedrooms, inhale the food out of our refrigerators, and hog our remote controls—don't grade our lives on a curve. When they see us mess up, you can be sure they're taking notes. That's why we must make every effort to model exemplary character.

Sure, all of us let them down somewhere along the way. We parents have a bad habit of being human. But our human frailties can never excuse us from daily monitoring our standards of integrity. The good news is that love covers a multitude of mistakes. The bad news is that if the mistakes are consistent and glaring enough, our children will be more inclined to follow our lead.

That's why we must embrace integrity if we ever want to transfer it to our children. It's a 24/7/365 assignment. Children led through life by mothers and fathers of integrity have it much easier when they become adults. Ethics aren't debatable. Truth isn't negotiable. Being honorable, reliable, and dependable is far more of a foregone conclusion when great character has been their consistent example throughout childhood. King Solomon said it well, "A righteous man who walks in his integrity—how blessed are his sons after him" (Proverbs 20:7 NIV).

Adapted from *Raising Kids Who Turn Out Right*

## 8

GIVE YOUR KIDS

# Love That Envisions
# a Hopeful Future

*Anything*—minus *hope*—equals *nothing*. Hope is like oxygen when it comes to a person's ability to live effectively. Take it away, and everything else becomes irrelevant. Without a confidence that God has the future under control, it is impossible to live a contented life. Far worse, without divine hope people surrender too soon and die too young.

Parents who want to raise children into strong, confident, resilient adults must grasp the reality of their children's fundamental need for a strong hope. But understanding this reality is only half of the equation. We also need to understand where *grace* fits in. You see, grace and hope are kissing cousins. When children receive something that they know is given at a high cost, it bolsters their confidence that there are things in life worth hoping for. Kids groomed with hope that is tempered with grace find it far easier to dream, to trust, and to long for a greater good.

Parents who make genuine hope an anchor tenet of their souls become better, more satisfied people and far more effective parents—period.

That's because God has placed us as lights on a hill for our families. It is our job to send out clear signals that help our children get their bearings, keep their wits, and navigate the future. We're to be there to *warn them* away from the rocks and shallow shoals. We're to be there to *guide them* safely back into the center of the channel when they've drifted off course. We are a *lighthouse*, permanently established to show them the way through the turbulent years of childhood and into the deep blue waters of tomorrow.

If dreams are made of sand, then hope is made of concrete. It's the bulkhead that withstands the pounding waves of life's stormy seas. It's the belief that tomorrow is worth facing. But it must have a divine touch to last. Hope that is a product of human wisdom is temporal at best. Those who allow God's love to cast its cross–shaped shadow over their human spirits give hope eternal life.

Adapted from *Grace-Based Parenting*

50 Ways to Really Love Your Kids

# Give Your Kids a Love
# That Models
# True Greatness

• • • • •

When all the people were being
baptized by John, Jesus also was baptized.
While Jesus was praying,
heaven opened and the Holy Spirit came
down on him in the form of a dove.
Then a voice came from heaven, saying,

*"You are my Son, whom I love,
and I am very pleased with you."*

Luke 3:21-22 NCV

Dr. Tim Kimmel

## 9

## GIVE YOUR KIDS

# Love That Models True Greatness

It's really quite simple. Our kids are going to end up *somewhere*. We're going to aim them at *something*. Why not aim them at true *greatness*? What's that? It's a life committed to loving God and serving others with a whole heart. When you think of the alternatives, why not aim your kids at something that lasts forever?

I know what you're thinking. *I can't do that. I don't have what it takes.*

What's the matter? Are you thinking about those feet of clay you put your shoes over today? Don't worry about that, God has been using the weak to confound the wise since the beginning of time. What about those regrets? How about once and for all letting God dispose of them?

Yeah, but you say, "I'm still weighed down with inadequacies, limited knowledge, and flawed experiences, and I can't seem to get a grip on those fears that lurk in the corners of my conscience." All I know is that God draws straight lines with crooked sticks all the time. Besides, raising kids for greatness is far less about what you do and far more about what you are. Our kids just need an idea of what greatness looks like, feels like, tastes like, smells like, and sounds like. And you can do all of that by practicing one quality: grace—treating others the way God treats you.

Let grace permeate the pores of your life. Let it seep through your intellect, volition, emotions, and spirit. Let it be the posture of your heart, the purpose of your hands, and the expression upon your face. If your kids experience this grace every day, grooming them for greatness will be easy.

God did a great forgiveness for you. He did a great transformation in you. And He wants to do a great work through you. Let Him squeeze all the self, confusion, second-guessing, and fear out of you. In its place let the attitude of a *great* parent shine in everything you do.

Love big! Work hard! Forgive gladly! Repent quickly! Encourage graciously! Speak humbly! Play enthusiastically! Think abundantly! Serve eagerly! Worship earnestly! And . . . never stop dancing!

Adapted from *Raising Kids for True Greatness*

# 10

## Love That Finds Its Source in God

Solving a division problem requires finding a common denominator. Raising kids who sense an overwhelming love from their parents also requires finding commonality. May I suggest a factor that works every time? It is parents who live with the understanding that God *is* their life.

They don't prioritize life like so many people do: God, my spouse, my kids, my friends, my work, my church, etc. No. Their list goes more like this: there's God, and then there's God and my spouse, God and my kids, God and my friends, God and my work, God and my church, God and my joys, God and my setbacks, God and every person and challenge I encounter each day. When kids are brought up with parents whose hearts beat for God's glory, they are far more inclined to grow up to have hearts that beat for Him too.

If we genuinely want to build kids who live abundant lives as adults we must *show* them what this looks like. We can't assign this job to the religious professionals. The primary responsibility falls on us as ambassadors of God's love, power, and grace. When it's real in us, our kids don't miss it.

Regardless of the make and model of your heart, God can still use you. He calls the rank and file to greatness, the obscure to notoriety, the weak to victory, and the crippled and lonely to the finish line. With Him we're everything; without Him we don't have a prayer.

We need to show our sons and daughters how to let God's power burn in their souls. It will help them develop the ability to resist scorn and the wisdom to draw near to people who share their common faith. By embracing an abiding confidence in God, their lives can stand out in more ways than you can count. They will prove that you don't need glamour to be attractive, or influential friends to be significant, or money to be wealthy, or muscles to be strong, or academic degrees to be wise, or titles to have an impact . . . and you don't need to be tall to be looked up to.

These are just some of the many ways that life falls into place when we find its source in God.

Adapted from *Homegrown Heroes* and *Raising Kids for True Greatness*

## GIVE YOUR KIDS

# Love That Admits Mistakes

If you feel like you should be in the line for parents who have really blown it, you'll have to get in line behind me. We've all fallen short. We've stolen our children's joy more times than we'd like to count. We've turned non–issues into crises, sculpted molehills into mountains, even reached inside our children's tender hearts and pinched them simply because we could.

God is in the forgiveness business. He loves to get out the sponge and clean the chalkboard filled with the marks that have accumulated against us. There's a price for this, but it was one He was willing to pay on our behalf.

If you're like me, you need to hear Him say, "It's all right. I forgive you. I'll help you recover from the mistakes you've made with your kids." It starts by asking Him for this gift. Ask Him to help you meet the deep, driving inner needs of your child. Tell Him how much you want to pass on to your children not only love, but a secure love that can go with them all the way through their lives. He's the great *forgiver.* That's what He's all about.

One more thing: you will need to ask your children's forgiveness, too. It takes courage to accept blame, to admit that you are wrong. It takes courage to swallow your pride, to fork down plates full of "crow," and to submit to the consequences.

The timid wimps of life stand and fight for their misguided pride and inexcusable actions. They pass the buck and make scapegoats of the innocent. A courageous parent faces those he has wronged and openly admits he let them down. When you admit you are wrong to your three–year–old boy, his eyes may fill with tears. But don't assume they are tears of shame. Far from it! They are tears of pride and confidence in a parent who is not afraid to face personal faults with courage.

*Above all, love each other deeply because love covers over a multitude of sins.*

1 PETER 4:8 NIV

Adapted from *Grace-Based Parenting* and *Basic Training for a Few Good Men*

## Give Your Kids

# Love That Thinks Abundantly

*Abundant thinkers.* I love those words—especially when they are put side–by–side to describe the most positive type of parent any child could grow up with.

*Abundant thinkers.* These two words are more than kissing cousins, they are conjoined twins. Parents who embody this way of thinking when it comes to how they treat each other, their kids, and everyone they encounter create one of the best environments for setting kids up for greatness in every dimension of their adult lives.

Abundant thinkers are folks who are fun to be around, enjoyable to work with, and usually easier to look at. Because fear doesn't run their lives and they view anxiety as something to mastered, they tend to show a lot less wear and tear on their faces. They are happy, positive people who maintain a generous attitude toward life. Kids who grow up around mothers and fathers who smile a lot, cheer a lot, sing a lot, dance a lot, dream a lot, and laugh a lot find it so much easier to be like that themselves.

I get such a kick out of watching these kinds of parents in action. They start with the presupposition that all the good things in life have no boundaries. That inclines them to hold everything they have in open hands.

These are the kinds of parents who are a blast to vacation with. They're also handy to have nearby when you're facing a crisis. They're deliberate, balanced, and cool–headed under pressure. Come to think of it, they're fun to have dinner with. Rumor says they're pretty comfortable to wake up next to, also. It's probably no surprise that these kinds of parents are fueled by a God who came to give us life and give it more abundantly (John 10:10).

Abundant thinking. Why don't you make it your aim? Sit back and enjoy seeing its impact. It's a way of life that will fill your child's sails with the kind of exhilarating wind that can propel them to the deeper waters of adulthood with far more enthusiasm.

Adapted from *Raising Kids for True Greatness*

# 13

## Love That Keeps Forever in Mind

The fact that infinite space surrounds us all the time isn't a coincidence.

It's a reminder.

It prompts us to consider that everything in life takes on a different perspective when weighed against the backdrop of eternity. You name it. Relationships, accomplishments, even disappointments look different when we put them through the filter of forever.

This perspective is the key to peace and contentment. If forgiveness gives us the ability to love and clear boundaries outline a crystallized purpose, then an eternal perspective gives us solid hope. That's why shrewd parents throw the experiences of the day up against the infinite backdrop of God's bigger plan. The highs and lows of our children's days make more sense when we remind them of their eternal legacy. They need to know that they are not chance happenings on a planet with no purpose. Today was no accident. Tomorrow is part of forever.

Without an eternal perspective we're forced to evaluate everything that happens to us according to arbitrary and superficial standards. Our worth becomes an issue of achievement. Satisfaction becomes an issue of acquisition. We end up trading living for longing, happiness for hurriedness, and true rest for anxiety. When this life is all that we have going for us, we're forced to grab all the gusto we can—as quickly as we can.

What we need is the ability to make choices that don't jeopardize eternal relationships for temporary rewards. An eternal perspective helps us do that. Parents who recognize that relationships are more important than personal gain or personal satisfaction have a better chance of maintaining a heart connection to their children. They run their daily decisions through a grid that would never allow something that lasts for a moment, or even a lifetime, to take priority over a person who lasts forever.

One simple principle captures it all: *Never sacrifice the permanent on the altar of the immediate.* Keep those words on the front side of everything you do, and your kids will get a lot more mileage for their lives. Come to think of it, so will you—all the way to forever.

Adapted from *Little House on the Freeway*

# 14

## GIVE YOUR KIDS

# Love That Always Sees Their True Potential

Comparison is the poison pill of parenting. It not only kills your joy, it snuffs out your ability to mine the ore of potentiality that has been placed deep inside your "average" child—a child who happens to be made in God's image.

What makes it all worse is the painful reality that our children realize it anytime we let ourselves compare our kids to the airbrushed ideals that our culture celebrates. They get the gut–level feeling that they've fallen short of our hopes for them.

It's easy to trip into this trap. We live in the secular context of a 24/7 worship service that sings praises to beauty, talent, and accomplishments. And often a good friend, grandparent, or older sibling is the one leading the cultural praise choir. Batting averages, GPAs, runway model looks, test scores, dress sizes, and major awards become the unconscious grading scale. And even though only a precious few meet these standards, they nevertheless become the benchmarks for too many disappointed parents . . . and kids.

Stop for a second. Step back. Take in the BIG picture. Who's the mastermind behind the comparison compulsion of the world system anyway? Last time I checked, it was the lying snake that slithered into Eden. In all this time he hasn't changed his tune. His lies about what's important are still lies, even if an entire generation embraces them with all they've got.

Then there is another voice whispering your name. Even though the culture may try to drown Him out, His voice still cuts through the clamor of comparison. He reminds us that our children are born with a gnawing need *to matter*. It's a sense of purpose that comes from being one of God's amazing works of art. He means for everyone's potential to be realized and developed. That is the very voice that longs to echo in our hearts when we look at our kids. He wants us to see with His eyes and realize just how extraordinary our struggling, average kids really are.

Adapted from *"Extraordinarily Average"*

# 15

# Love That Manages Their Doubts

Doubts are part of life. They especially like to haunt our children. To help them galvanize their faith, we each must live a life that doesn't doubt in the shadows what God has made clear in the light.

I am reminded of some advice King George VI of England gave to a worried and doubtful empire. To put his words in context I need to take you to London, Christmas Eve, 1939. It was the king's annual Christmas speech. He wanted to bring his loyal subjects a message of cheer and encouragement. But it was difficult. Across the English Channel and within the very heart of Europe, the poison of Nazi Germany was spilling through the lowlands, Poland, and across the Rhine. Hitler's goal was clear: he wanted to own Europe.

It was obvious to everyone that England presented Hitler's biggest challenge. His goals for greater Europe could not be met without first bringing the British Empire to its knees. Everyone knew it was just a matter of time before the German *Luftwaffe* would darken the skies over London and rain its deadly bombs on the British people.

To offer hope in the midst of despair and courage in the face of certain calamity, King George borrowed a quote from a woman named Mini Louise Haskin. Her words that he shared in his Christmas address were the most appropriate words anyone could offer at the threshold of war. They also are the best advice I know for conscientious parents wanting to raise faithful kids in the midst of a culture of doubt. King George said:

> "I said to the man who stood at the gate of the year, 'Give me a light that I may tread safely into the unknown.' And he replied, 'Go into the darkness and put your hand into the hand of God. That shall be to you better than light and safer than the known way.' "
>
> Profound words then; powerful words now.

Adapted from *Why Christian Kids Rebel*

# 16

## GIVE YOUR KIDS

# Love That Remains Calm While Their Faith is on Trial

Father and daughter, the Poconos, Christmas break, many years ago. The scene couldn't have been more picturesque. The mood couldn't have been more satisfying. We were driving parallel to a river through a tunnel of trees. The leftover autumn leaves whipped up behind us as we rode along in silence. I was contented with my world.

My daughter, Karis, broke the silence. "Daddy, what if it's not true?"

I looked at her. "What if what's not true, honey?"

"What if all the stuff about Jesus and the Bible isn't true?"

All my internal alarms went off at once. The day suddenly turned cold. Every instinct pushed me to grab my Bible and do a full court press on her belief system. But this wasn't the time or the place. A little girl was asking an honest question. She needed a response . . . not a reaction.

I pulled our car over to the side of the road and sat quietly for a moment, breathing a quick prayer, trying to determine the best way to approach her question.

She decided to elaborate. "What I mean is . . . well, I was wondering how we can know for certain if all of the stories about the Bible are true. But I've been worried that doubting is wrong."

"No Karis, doubting isn't wrong. It's human. I've had doubts before. Lots of them. That's why it all comes down to faith. God gives us enough evidence and enough information to make educated decisions. But He doesn't fill in all of the blanks. He leaves just enough room for us to have to make a choice to trust. I'm not concerned that you might occasionally doubt. I'll only be concerned if you let your doubts run your life."

The life of faith isn't a done deal just because our kids prayed a prayer one day. It's a walk, a lifelong journey toward God. Our job of modeling it is never over. And as we live it out each day, we find that we, too, benefit from the promise: "He is a rewarder of those who diligently seek Him" (Hebrews 11:6 NKJV).

Adapted from *Raising Kids Who Turn Out Right*

## GIVE YOUR KIDS

# Love That Encourages a Life of Adventure

A good childhood is meant to be lived large, loud, and loaded with reasonable risks. It's a life of adventure that maximizes the potential God has placed in the hearts and minds of our children. Early days marked by mighty quests tap our children's intellects, challenge their physical capabilities, temper their emotions, and galvanize their courage. And while we're on the subject, children need to live a great spiritual adventure too—one that forces them to truly trust God and see with their own eyes just how big and wonderful He really is.

Here's the problem. If parents were to lick their index fingers and hold them to the prevailing winds of popular opinion, they'd get the clear sense that their job is to raise *safe* kids.

What a shame.

*Shame?* What's wrong with wanting to raise a safe kid? Simple. It's often the very attitude that blocks us from raising a *strong* one.

A qualification is in order. There's nothing wrong with wanting to know the who, what, where, why, how, and when of our children's lives. There's nothing wrong with restricting or even vetoing some of their ideas when it is obvious they are too naïve to see the threats that surround them. And let's hear a round of applause for seatbelts, bike helmets, and kneepads. What I've just cataloged are items from the standard list of responsible parenting. To do less would be reckless.

But there is a force that pulls us toward protecting our children too much. It's a force that unwittingly causes us to handicap their potential. That force is called *fear*. It's too easy to let it define us. Fear–based parenting is good at producing safe kids. Unfortunately, it's also good at producing pushovers and spiritual sissies. It leaves children weak, timid, and at the mercy of life.

There's a balance between recklessness and fear. It's called a life of adventure. It's the best way to raise a strong kid. Oh, I forgot to mention something. When you raise a strong kid, you also get a safe one thrown in . . . free of charge.

## 18

GIVE YOUR KIDS

# Love That Encourages Their Best

Welcome to the graceful middle ground between mediocrity and perfection. It's a haven that is tailor–made for kids who want to feel a balanced love deep down in their bones. Those who get to enjoy it throughout childhood find that eventually it fits like a well–worn pair of boots. And it has an uncanny way of sending them into adulthood with a comfortable contentment about their potential. It's that happy medium between the toxic extremes of human capabilities that helps children *put forth their best efforts*.

Mediocrity is the love child of laziness. It's what children end up with when they have been allowed—or worse, encouraged—to consistently take the path of least resistance. Perfectionism, on the other hand, exacts far too high of a price. It may be achieved, and it might even come with some nice rewards, but it can never be enjoyed. That's because perfectionism usually comes drenched in years of tears.

Then there's this balanced option, this bubble–in–the–middle commitment that enables kids to really hit their sweet spot . . . it's simply called "their best." It's far nobler to build this into them than mediocrity, and it's far more rewarding than perfectionism could ever be. Helping children develop a lifelong commitment to do their best yields a satisfaction that tends to take center stage in their hearts. That's because doing their best requires that they learn how to manufacture that internal oil that lubricates a life of success—sweat. And sweat isn't always that salty stuff they wash off in the shower. Sometimes it seeps from the pores of their emotional, intellectual, and even spiritual systems. When it comes from these compartments of their lives it goes by other names like tenacity, grit, backbone, and determination. But it is no less rewarding.

Mediocrity, perfectionism, doing their best. Each exacts a price from a parent. The first pays off in years of regret. The second returns years of resentment. The third—that commitment to helping your kids do their best—brings years of reward and relief . . . for you, for them, and for all the people on the receiving end of your loving efforts.

## 19

## GIVE YOUR KIDS

# Love That Doesn't Circumvent Consequences

It's difficult to determine how you can take a decade or so of character training and blow it all in one afternoon, but I managed to. I was thirteen. It was winter. My friend and I were bored.

I don't recall who came up with the idea. It doesn't matter. Whether you're the architect of a crime or merely an accessory doesn't make your actions any more or less stupid. The target was a slot machine. The plan was to play it. The problem was that it was locked in a private summer cottage. We took all the money we had (about $3), cashed it into nickels, and headed for our appointment with destiny.

The lock . . . a piece of cake. The slot machine . . . a lot of fun . . . until it had managed to win back all of its money as well as ours. We left the way we came, only three dollars poorer.

Two county policemen were waiting for us. Someone had phoned us in. They immediately called our fathers. My friend's father was a state trooper. "Send him home. I'll deal with him." Read: *Don't embarrass me!* My father was called. After inquiring of the consequences and learning that I would be processed, he said two words: "Process him!"

This involved a trip to the local precinct, questioning about unsolved crimes, and healthy humiliation. But it worked. I never did anything stupid like that again. My friend—the one whose father circumvented the process for him—he's been in the state penitentiary . . . twice.

Bottom line: Don't circumvent the negative consequences of your children's foolish actions. If you do, you only set them up for greater heartache. Kids do stupid things. They embarrass us. They let us down. When they do, we have a strategic responsibility to deal with them in such a way that allows the consequences of their foolishness to come down on their heads hard enough to knock some sense into them. My father loved me enough to let me feel the full extent of my actions. He hated the thought of me making crime a passion even more than he hated the personal embarrassment he'd have to endure in church when word got around that Howard Kimmel's son, Tim, happened to be a jerk.

And I'm a better man for it.

Adapted from *"My Criminal Record"*

## 20

## GIVE YOUR KIDS

# Love That Places High Value on Wisdom

Certain life skills get our children farther along the road to success than others. They also empower our kids to play far more strategic roles in the larger family of man. For instance, teaching children the benefit of putting higher value on others than they do on themselves inclines them to look out for the weak and disenfranchised people they encounter each day. Showing them the benefit of hard work turns them into lifelong assets rather than daily liabilities.

But there is one life skill that we don't want to fail to give them. That's because once they have it, this skill automatically enhances all of the others. I'm talking about being a *wisdom hunter*.

They're not born with this skill. Their I. Q. has no bearing on it. And children certainly don't develop this skill by accident. On the contrary, the commitment to pursuing wisdom is a deliberate decision. And this determination is much easier to make when it's spawned within the hearts of loving parents who want to raise kids who will make the world better.

All we're talking about here are parents who strive to teach their children how to turn knowledge into practical life skills. That's all wisdom is—information with the ability to utilize it effectively. The prerequisite for a wisdom hunter is an overriding fear of God. That's where the trail begins. Proverbs 9:10 reminds us that the fear of God is the *beginning* of wisdom.

Unfortunately, raising wisdom hunters isn't in vogue among a lot of parents. Sociologist Allen Bloom put his hand on the pulse of this issue. His words are achingly true:

"Fathers and mothers have lost the idea that the highest aspiration they might have for their children is for them to be wise—as priests, prophets, or philosophers are wise. Specialized competence and success are all that they [most fathers and mothers] can imagine."[1]

We can aim higher. We *must* aim higher. And in the process, we'll raise kids who end up leaving the world nicer, safer, and far better than they found it—wisdom hunters who simply take after their parents.

Adapted from *Grace-Based Parenting*

50 Ways to Really Love Your Kids

# Give Them a Love That Reveres God's Word

• • • • •

Those who love your teachings

will find true peace,

and nothing will defeat them.

PSALM 119:165 NCV

Since you were a child you have known

the Holy Scriptures which are able

to make you wise. And that wisdom leads to

salvation through faith in Christ Jesus.

2 TIMOTHY 3:15 NCV

Dr. Tim Kimmel

## 21

GIVE YOUR KIDS

# Love That Reveres God's Word

"I saw the movie *The Bible*, and I loved it so much that I bought the book."

It's an old joke, but hidden within it is a weighty clue for transferring a calm and assuring love to our children's hearts. It happens when we love them enough to revere the very voice of the God who gifted them to us and assigned us the honor of giving their lives meaning. It's a tall order, but doable. But we're kidding ourselves if we think we can fulfill it without His help.

Our success pivots on the level of sophistication of our faith.

Faith thrives on a regular intake of God's Word. Sunday morning messages and group studies are part of the equation. But they aren't enough. We need fresh strength each day. That's why we must commit to a daily ingestion of God's Word.

I'm not legalistic about *how*. I'm not legalistic about *when*. I'm just realistic. I'm realistic enough to know I can't expect my faith to be strong and vital if I deny it the food it needs to thrive.

Faith needs the Word of God.

For years I played games with this issue. I began the habit of studying the Bible only to let it slip away. I did a lot of rationalizing about how busy my life was and how often I heard the scriptures taught at church. But all my rationalizations were just empty excuses.

At last I had to confront myself with the unvarnished truth: I had plenty of time for the things I felt were important. So why didn't I have time for God's Word? Simple. I didn't think it was important enough. Which meant that I didn't think *God* was important enough. Which meant the best interests of my wife and my children were not important enough.

Life is tough enough *with* regular doses of God's truth. It's impossible to figure out without it. Our kids will value only what we value. That's why we do ourselves a favor, and we give our children a solid gold foundation, when we keep our hearts connected to God through the daily lifeline of His Word.

Adapted from Raising Kids Who Turn Out Right

## 22

GIVE YOUR KIDS

# Love That Believes in the Power of Prayer

Prayer. Of all the weapons handed to us to protect our children, this is one of the most powerful. For most people, prayer doesn't need proof; it just needs practice. Parents wanting to pass on an unwavering love to their children need to enter into this haven of rest regularly.

I know one mom who did it, and her son will never be the same.

The story slips from the shadows of one of Korea's darkest hours and a place called Heartbreak Ridge. It got its name from the violent battles fought near its peak. Too often, it was bathed in the blood and tears of countless American soldiers.

One night the battle was unusually intense. The North Koreans, firmly dug into the rocky terrain, used their home court advantage to keep the night skies lit with flares and the air filled with the hot death of machine gun fire.

An American soldier worked his way through the maze of enemy emplacements only to be struck down about fifty meters beyond the enemy's outer lines. From the darkness he screamed in pain, begging for someone to rescue him. Nobody moved.

Another young man, crouched in a foxhole, kept his head down but kept lifting his wrist up into the light given off by the flares. Suddenly he bolted through the enemy fire, grabbed his wounded comrade, and raced him back through the violence to the safety of an American foxhole.

His lieutenant crawled over to find out what gave him the sudden urge for heroics.

"It wasn't heroics, Sir. And it really wasn't a risk," the young man replied. "I kept checking my watch until I knew it was nine o'clock back at my home in Kansas. You see, Sir, before I left home my mother told me, 'Son, every morning at nine o'clock, I'll be praying for you.' I knew that God would protect me."

Do you want to give your children rest for their spirits? Be a parent who prays for them every day. Who knows? It just might save their lives . . . or someone else's.

Adapted from *Little House on the Freeway*

## 23

## GIVE YOUR KIDS

# Love That Rests on Clear Moral Boundaries

Do you know the main thing I appreciate about *truth*? It's the fact that regardless of whether you like it or not, there's nothing you can do about it.

Truth *is*. Obviously I'll get an argument from the leading voices for conventional wisdom. But the last time I checked, conventional wisdom is generally just a notch or two above the polling of the ignorant. The prevailing assumption of our enlightened society is that there is no such thing as absolute truth. They would like us to believe that God didn't hand Moses Ten Commandments carved in stone, He gave him Ten Suggestions written in pencil.

Forget the fact that the whole scientific community rests on certain non–negotiable laws. And let's not overlook the reality that from mathematics to medicine we would not be able to function five minutes were it not for the presence of realities that are both inescapable and absolute.

God didn't establish the universe on absolute truths and then decide to arbitrarily skip over the whole area of morality. He loves us too much to do that to us. And in this area of morality our love for our children must not falter. Our kids need to know that when it comes to the whole issue of right and wrong, there are definitely some things they can't do anything about. This includes the law of cause and effect. If you lie, people will stop believing in you. If you betray covenants, people will stop trusting you. If you're selfish, people will reject you.

Our kids need a moral compass that points to true north (God) in order to navigate the treacherous waters of contemporary culture. Without it kids get confused, frustrated, scared, and angry. But with it they are free to operate at their maximum potential. That's because truth sets you free (John 8:32).

Do you want your kids to win at life? Do you want them to excel at love? Of course you do. Then set them free by not only teaching them the things they can't do anything about, but by showing them what these truths look like modeled in your life.

## 24

## GIVE YOUR KIDS

# Love That Seeks
# God's Grand Purposes

One of the great debates in literature has to do with who came up with the best opening line to a book. Charles Dickens gets a lot of votes for his pithy start to *A Tale of Two Cities*. He summarized so much of the powerful story that followed when he said, "It was the best of times; it was the worst of times."

Another commanding opening line is the one you find at the front of Rick Warren's influential work, *The Purpose Driven Life*. Few books in history have captured the true essence of our relationship to God better than this one. And the four words set by themselves on the first line of the book summarize the heart of his message.

*It's not about you.*

Life isn't about you or me. It's not about our children or our plans for them. It is 100% and fundamentally about God. It's *all* about God . . . and *His* plans for us.

Since this is so, we do well to instill this truth into our children from the moment they take their first breath. That's because between the time of their first breath and their last, they are either going to be part of God's overarching plan for the world, or they are going to stand against it. Either way, the bigger story will never be about them. It will be about the Creator of their life and the true Author of the amazing story that God wants to make out of their life.

And that's exactly what God wants their life to be: an utterly *amazing* story. Obviously this reality is difficult to transfer in a theoretical fashion. Making God the source, the first, the last, and the center of their life doesn't sink in as a result of a few strategic pep talks around the dinner table. The preeminence of God is not discovered in part–time lessons but in real–time love. It is our personal excitement about being part of God's grand purposes that moves this desire from our children's heads to their hearts.

Which brings up another great opening line of a book: *In the beginning God . . .*

Adapted from *Raising Kids for True Greatness*

## 25

## GIVE YOUR KIDS

# Love That Is Others-Oriented

Just think, we're given almost two decades to have our children follow us around through life. That's twenty *years* of them watching us cross the paths of thousands of people from every rung on the social ladder, every score on the academic grading scale, and every color on the ethnic rainbow. Each encounter has something in common with the next—an opportunity to demonstrate the power found in valuing other people higher than yourself.

It's a God thing.

But it's certainly not a people thing. It's not even in the ballpark of basic human instincts. In fact, if anything, it runs counter to most of what our culture lives for. Sadly, too many people are enmeshed in the Cult of Self–Worship. The people who surround them are seen as appendages to their selfish agendas and extensions of their fragile egos.

The people trying to sell the world a hamburger realize this. That's why they're quick to chant: You! You're the one! We do it all for *you*!

If "Ole Blue Eyes," could weigh in on the subject, he'd do it *"My way!"*

Then there's God's way, an infinitely sounder plan to use His children to bring the best out of every person who crosses their paths.

That's where you and I fit in. We are blessed by our Creator with a chance to touch people's lives in a "forever" type of way simply by recognizing them as valued members of the human race. Our second blessing is that we get to transfer this others–orientated view of life to our kids.

True, some people are easier to value than others. And it's equally true that some might try to take advantage of our goodness. But that's God's problem. He'll sort it all out.

In the meantime, our sons and daughters gain a gift that will reward them all the way to the day they take their last breath. They'll never lack for friends and never long for a reason to get up in the morning. It's just another way loving parents leave a legacy that never dies.

## 26

GIVE YOUR KIDS

# Love That Applauds Great Effort

It's been a long time . . . a very long time . . . since I donned pads and cleats to play high school football. The other day while watching my son's practice I realized that little has changed over the years since I was where he was. It's still just a game of blocking, tackling, and falling forward. But there is one element that slipped into the playbook somewhere between the time I turned in my helmet and when they brought back the two–point conversion.

It's the "high five."

I see them everywhere. You've seen them too. You've done them. A fullback breaks for a thirty–yard gain. The quarterback catches up with him as he jumps to his feet, and . . . high five! It's a nonverbal "way to go!" . . . a reaction to a job well done. You don't have to *actually perform* a high five in order to experience a high–five moment. And I've noticed that parents who want to instill a confident love in their kids keep an eye out for these moments. Their praise comes naturally.

But you might be thinking, *"Tim, you have no idea how little we've had to applaud lately. We've got bills that we can't pay, a car that seldom starts, strep throat haunting our kids' bedrooms, a backed up septic tank, a leak in the roof, scary neighbors, goofy in–laws, a split in our church, a dog that is literally on his last legs, piranha in our birdbath, and company that won't leave. It's hard to see anything worth celebrating, even if it is about our kids."*

Oh, my friend, let me encourage you. These moments are *everywhere*. Like: their first tooth, first step, the first time they make their bed by themselves, that first bike ride without training wheels, the first verse they memorize, a job well done with the lawn mower. And we can't forget those moral choices: your daughter's commitment to modesty, your son sticking up for a girl's reputation in the locker room.

High fives. They get snapped around the throne room of heaven when God sees *you* put forth a good effort. When it comes to your kids, make applause a part of your heart, too.

Adapted from *"High Fives"*

## 27

## Give Your Kids

# Love That Prepares Them for Marriage

There's an old saying that goes, "You're either doubled or halved on your wedding day." When it's one of our kids making their way to the altar, we'd certainly vote for multiplication over division.

One of the greatest points of anxiety in the average person's life surrounds the process of courting, dating, and marrying who they hope is the right person. Most of this anxiety is either self–imposed, or pushed onto them by the shallow priorities of the culture that surrounds them. So much of the pain of this process can be eliminated in advance if children are properly prepared for marriage.

The key to the process isn't in finding the right mate. It's in being the right person.

I don't want to make this sound like it's a simple slam dunk, but it certainly isn't as difficult as most people make it. Once again, our culture takes something that God meant to be a rewarding part of everyone's life and complicates it beyond logic. It's just the obvious next step of our culture's needy nature. When people are encouraged to make themselves the center of their universe, we shouldn't be surprised to find faulty thinking about matrimony. Too often we seem bent on finding a person who meets our expectations and compliments our ego needs.

This is where we can save our children a lot of grief. We take the focus off of them finding the person who can complete them and instead refocus them on becoming the kind of person who automatically makes the one they marry much more valuable.

Having character, seeing others as more important than themselves, not being afraid of hard work, handling money properly, and mastering the art of fighting fair—this is the stuff that makes our children great assets on their wedding day. And here's the good news: these kinds of people tend to attract the same kind of people.

So . . . old sayings can be blunt, but they can also spare us some serious headaches if we're willing to learn from them. Think *multiplication*.

Adapted from *Raising Kids for True Greatness*

## 28

# Love That Respects God's Gift of Sex

One of the great gifts anyone can bring to his or her future spouse is showing up for the wedding sexually pure. If we as parents aim our kids at anything less, we not only show a lack of respect for God and His wonderful gift of sex, but a lack of respect for our children as well. Marriage is tough enough. Why add regret to their dowries?

At the same time, we don't want to make this goal of sexual purity an albatross around their necks. How do we hinder them like that? Simple: by articulating the goal, but doing little or nothing to help them reach it. Trying to enforce a high sexual standard is noble, but it doesn't always consider just how desperate their situations are.

It might help to know that the average teenage boy thinks about sex ALL THE TIME! The average teenage girl thinks about sex A LOT of the time. Our kids' hormones have a drug potency on par with heroin. And we shouldn't be fooled into thinking that raising our children in an environment that isolates them from sexual stimuli somehow wins the lion's share of the battle for them . . . or us. That's because the biggest battle for their purity rages *within* them. Lust wants to overtake them and control their thoughts and choices. This is where God's Spirit wants to step into the middle of the battle and give them the help they need to win it.

Sometimes all it takes to figure out what our children need when it comes to dealing with their sexual urges is to *have a good memory.* If all they know from us are lectures about purity and guilt trips when they struggle, their chances of achieving this goal go way down. We need to be engaged in a grace–based dialogue with them throughout their childhoods—especially their adolescent years.

Talk with them. Be honest and transparent with them. Pray with them; prepare them. Show understanding when they struggle. Applaud their victories. Who knows? It just might help you breathe a lot easier when you take your seat on their wedding day.

Adapted from *Raising Kids for True Greatness*

## 29

## GIVE YOUR KIDS

# Love That Holds Up Under Fire

It's never too early or too late to teach our kids the qualities they need to achieve true greatness. Sooner than we ever imagined our children slip out of our daily lives for good. Before they go, we need to make sure we've tucked examples of courage and endurance in their hearts.

We face myriad relational, spiritual, financial, physical, and moral battles. I've met many parents who are willing to sacrifice. Being willing is one thing; carrying it out is another matter. The fact is parenting is often a painful and lonely task. Most of the payoff is so far down the road that it's tempting to give up.

We must not.

You are Major Mom or Colonel Dad surrounded by some significant individuals who look a lot like you. They have enough of a belief in the things that really matter to be willing to join you on the battlefront. But these same people are threatened by the discouragement that slips through the cracks of their fragile spirits. The bursts from culture's mortars explode around them. The temptation to run, to take the easy way out, or to surrender to their moral enemies is an enticing option. They turn to you for their cues.

At this point, they need examples more than pep talks. You can write principles in the back pages of their Bibles, put checklists on the refrigerator doors, and wax eloquently around the dinner tables. But if they don't smell the gunpowder of battle experience on you, your rhetoric will be little more than empty nouns and verbs. Reality dictates that when it comes to courage, endurance, and holding up under pressure, you can't rally the troops by googling some slogans and emailing them around your kids' foxholes.

You must lead the charge.

Make your life an indisputable example of courageous living, and watch what happens. Behind the immature eyes, a young mind will be taking careful notes. From the midst of the confusion of childhood, a developing determination will draw confident conclusions. And within the magical world of a youthful heart, a spirit will be groomed for greatness.

Adapted from *Homegrown Heroes*

## 30

# Love That Lets Them Take Risks

When you look at how deceptive and dangerous life is at street level, it's no wonder many parents would prefer to raise their kids in spiritual bubbles. I certainly don't blame them. The risks are real. The human toll is high. And yet, raising kids without coaching them on how to process risks actually does more harm than good.

We all can take a lesson from the trees.

Have you ever heard of *Biosphere II*? It was one of those extravagant experiments designed to see if humans could sustain a livable existence in other parts of the universe. It involved building an elaborate glass bubble out in the desert and then placing within this closed system all of the ecological necessities required to sustain both the artificial environment and the human life living within it. The most important part of the experiment was the trees.

The trees not only had to produce fruit to eat and moisture to drink, but their most vital role was the production of oxygen. The best trees were selected and planted in the best soil. Based on the calculations, the trees should have produced more than enough oxygen. Seven scientists were moved in for a two–year stay. The doors were sealed.

The trees failed. They wilted, drooped, and struggled to thrive. Some fell over. Oxygen levels plunged so low that they had to pump in oxygen from the outside to keep the scientists alive. After it was all over, the scientists scratched their heads as to why the trees failed to flourish. An outside tree expert finally gave them the answer they were looking for.

They failed to include one all–important ingredient in their utopian bubble. There was no wind in there. Without wind, trees are wimps. It is contrary winds that force a tree's roots deep and make its framework supple.

In the same way, the contrary winds of culture force our children to appropriate the power of God's Spirit and claim the true authority of His mighty Word to survive.

It's got to be done gradually. It's got to be done carefully. But the important point is that it's got to be *done*.

Adapted from *Why Christian Kids Rebel*

# 31

# Love Committed to Resolving Conflict

If we don't deal with conflict, it will deal with us. Resentment is a slave master.

It controls, beats down, and demands too much. It overtaxes friendships, ruins special events, and makes our kids' lives miserable. It even can cost us a good review at work. Unresolved anger inclines us to prejudge new relationships, withdraw from people who need us, and neutralize God's influence in our lives.

Lingering conflict can take its toll on our bodies, too. It might reward us with a miserable night's sleep or the curse of sleeping alone . . . for a long time. It's been known to spoil appetites or drive people to eat too much. Open-ended anger festers in some people's hearts to such a sad degree that it guarantees them a rough ride to the morgue, possibly sooner than later.

It's easy to read other people's minds. All I have to do is read my own. You're thinking of the pain that you've endured—pain that seems too intense to forgive. I know how you feel. I think of people who've had fun at my expense, who have attempted to move up the career ladder by trying to climb over me and then kick me off.

I think of friends who said they'd be there—and weren't. I've felt the cold steel of betrayal slipping into my back. And I've experienced that empty feeling that overwhelms you when you realize the hand shoving in the knife belongs to someone who should know better.

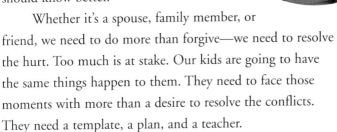

Whether it's a spouse, family member, or friend, we need to do more than forgive—we need to resolve the hurt. Too much is at stake. Our kids are going to have the same things happen to them. They need to face those moments with more than a desire to resolve the conflicts. They need a template, a plan, and a teacher.

We must turn the resolving of conflict into a skill.

Our love can show them how. The advice is cheap; the determination to take it is steep. But our kids are worth it. How about it? Bury the hatchet. Bury the handle. While you're at it, forget where you buried it.

Adapted from *Little House on the Freeway*

## 32

# Love That Refuses to Compare

Watch out! Our culture has a poison pill. It's called *comparison*. In its basic form it causes a material "bad trip". Swallow it too often and you're sure to get hooked. You end up with an addiction to things that don't last and a craving for things that don't really matter. It causes you to depend upon tomorrow to bring you the happiness that today can never supply.

God knew we were prone to this problem. That's why He closed off His list of the "Top Ten Principles for Effective Living and Loving" with this one: *Don't covet.*

Now *there's* a nasty word for you. Its synonyms are bad, too: *envy, jealousy, lust,* and *greed.* It starts in our hearts as a seed but gets watered and fertilized by the inevitable pressures on our pride. Your neighbor gets a promotion with a significant pay raise—the seed germinates. The new models roll into the showroom at the car dealerships—the seed drops roots. Your best friend, unlike you, still fits beautifully into dresses that are the same size she wore when she got married fifteen years ago. Ah, the seed is starting to sprout above the surface of your personality.

The next thing you know, you're a card–carrying member of the "If only . . . " club. *If only* I had a better job, a bigger house, a thinner waist, a bigger chest, a different husband/wife, a lifestyle like . . . *If only* I hadn't run up so many debts, neglected my spouse, quit that job, sold that stock, bought that stock. Here's the worst one: *If only* my kids were . . . or had . . . or . . . Well, you get the idea.

Sometimes we need to take inventory. Two questions: 1. Do you have a *personal* arrangement with the God of the universe? 2. Do you have children? Then I have great news . . . you're RICH. You're joint heirs with the Son of God which means that the universe already belongs to you. On top of that, you have a chance to pass on a love to your children that is going to last *forever*. Count your blessings and enjoy your wealth! It's the best poison prevention you can provide for your kids.

Adapted from *Little House on the Freeway*

## 33

GIVE YOUR KIDS

# Love That Allows Them to Be Different

When God was assigning children to you and me, I'll bet He had a grin on His face. He had to be excited about the unique qualities He had programmed into their DNA. After we actually got to see these qualities up close, however, it's not uncommon to wonder if that wasn't actually a smirk on His face.

Do some things about your kids drive you crazy? Do your kids sometimes annoy you or embarrass you? So do mine. It's very easy to assume that these characteristics automatically represent fundamental flaws in them.

Not necessarily.

Sometimes there's no moral or biblical problem with the things about our children that press our buttons. They're just *different*. One of the great characteristics of grace-based love is that it doesn't create moral issues out of things that are merely unconventional. Even more, it never uses the Bible or God's name to ridicule something about a child that is—when you look at it objectively—an amoral quality that just happens to drive us nuts!

Let me give you some words that often describe our children's distinctive qualities: *weird, bizarre, strange, goofy,* and *quirky.* Guess what? God made our kids that way. He actually likes them like that . . . and He wants us to like them that way, too. When we do, we give our children a gift that isn't forthcoming in most homes; we give them the freedom to be *different.*

It's one of the highest forms of grace. Letting children be unique goes contrary to so many parents. But when we do, we free our children to develop their one–of–a–kind styles of life. Let's not forget the obvious: they're children. They're young. Their hearts stir with an almost miraculous sense of wonder. Their imaginations often run wild and sometimes crazy gauntlets. God made them this way. It's a good thing.

I know, I know . . . you're thinking about your friends. What are they going to think of you as parents? I've got some good advice if that's the case. Do your kids a favor. Get new friends!

Adapted from *Grace-Based Parenting*

## 34

GIVE YOUR KIDS

# Love That Thrives on Laughter

Few things are more rewarding than growing up in a home filled with laughter. I'm not talking about that smoke–and–mirrors type of humor with its polite smiles and canned jokes. No, no. What I'm visualizing is that trigger–happy laughter that springs from the depths of a heart spilling over with genuine happiness.

You're thinking, "Is it possible to have this without first completely disconnecting from reality?" Let's face it. Life can be vicious. Many things in a typical family's life steal joy. I know what you're talking about. After all, where's the humor in our kids being sick or our jobs being insecure?

Obviously, there's nothing funny about the harsh realities of life. But laughter isn't about circumstances—it's about the filters through which you run your circumstances. These filters determine the attitudes we are going to process life with. And when you have the right filters, you not only find a lot to be thankful for, but a lot to laugh about.

Let's not forget that we're made in God's image. He is far more about laughter than we give Him credit for. Here's a truth that we need to prop up in the corner of this discussion:

all cultures and all people groups *laugh*. Why? It's a God thing. And when we make joy, happiness, and laughter anchor tenets of our children's lives, it's a God thing too.

During my childhood, I recall that some of the most enjoyable dinners were with my Jewish neighbors. They laughed a lot. Yet on their walls were pictures of family members who lost their lives in Hitler's camps. It had only happened a few years earlier. The words of the late comedian Red Skelton come to mind. He said, "I laugh so much to keep from crying."

Our children are facing a future that is going to work overtime to wipe the laughter off of their faces. A childhood of genuine happiness is the best way to keep that smile right where it is.

# 35

# Love That Carefully Stewards Their Tears

Tears are a gift. Those wet, thick, salty drops of emotion that slip from our children's eyes and slide down the front of their faces offer parents an unusual opportunity to build a solid love into the deeper crevices of their hearts. Everything pivots on how we view their tears and what we do about them.

Tears are one of two release valves that God has provided for our children's emotions. The other is laughter. Kind parents create an environment where there is an adequate outlet for both. But tears require special handling. They come from a container marked "Fragile" deep inside our children's hearts. God wants us to handle them with care.

That's easy when they are tears of joy or relief. Most homes have rooms already made up for these emotional guests. But what about the tears of sadness, loss, or fear? These call for a careful and well-positioned grace from Mom and Dad.

Sometimes our perch as adults causes us to view tears from a perspective that trivializes them. The death of a pet hamster or the disappointment over not being able to go on

"Mr. Toad's Wild Ride" can be written off easily when weighed against the bigger "do or die" issues of life. Our daughter's sadness over being rejected by a boy in her third–grade class can be dismissed as meaningless puppy love. But it's not meaningless to her. The fact that your five–year–old son's best friend moved away might not show up on your internal Richter scale, but he was your son's *best* friend.

Kids don't want us to trivialize their tears; they want us to respect them. When we respect *all* of their tears, they're more inclined to shed the more vulnerable brand around us—tears of shame and regret. Gentle, understanding shoulders that are ready to soak in these more *dangerous* tears put us in the best position to help them deal with what caused them.

I'll say it again, "Tears are a gift." Parents who *really* love their kids make childhood a safe place to let them flow.

# 36

GIVE YOUR KIDS

# Love That Maintains Moral Equilibrium

As blizzards go, it was huge. When my brother and I woke up and looked out our windows, all we saw was money. That's what we knew would be bulging in our pockets after spending all day shoveling out our neighbors. But we knew from experience that before we could hit the paying customers, we'd have to dig out the list of senior citizens our mother would hand to us on our way out the door.

Which brought us to Mrs. Martin's house. She was a widow and a waif of a woman, and when she answered the door, we knew something was seriously wrong. The hoarse voice that came from beneath the shaking layers of clothes was clue number one. The deathly quiet house was the other. The electric company had turned off her power.

The reasons why aren't important. What happened next is. While my brother started shoveling her sidewalk, I doubled back home to tell my father. He didn't hesitate. He didn't call the pastor for advice. He didn't get out his Bible for guidance. He just told me to get his insulated wire cutters while he put on his winter gear. Five minutes later, I watched this man who taught me to always respect authority snip the electric company's tag that promised criminal prosecution if tampered with, pull off the meter, remove the block, shove in the meter, and throw the main switch. Next he disappeared into her basement and lit the pilot on her furnace. Mrs. Martin would be safe and warm soon.

He showed me that in life, virtues sometimes collide. Occasionally you get a grand total of a split second to decide between doing the honorable thing and doing the correct thing, between doing what's good and doing what is best. Raising kids often puts us in conflicts between justice or mercy, holding the line and exercising latitude, running interference or letting them face the music. I've noticed that parents who know how to choose properly in those situations are the ones who have God's Word fresh in their mind every day and a good set of calluses on their knees.

Moral equilibrium: it's the universal cure for cold neighbors and confused hearts.

Adapted from *"When Virtues Collide"*

## 37

GIVE YOUR KIDS

# Love That Spills Over With Gratefulness

"Say *thank you.*" How many times have you had to remind your children to offer those two precious words? Don't be shocked if you're still whispering that suggestion in their ears long after they should know better.

It's too bad but also too true that people aren't born with a bent toward gratefulness. In fact, it's just the opposite. In spite of all they have, and all they've been given, too many people simply aren't satisfied. I'll take it a sad step further. They often feel like they're *entitled* to more. Lacking any sense of humility or graciousness, they believe they deserve the best seat in the house, the best office, the first place in line, the least amount of hassle, the biggest piece of the pie, the last piece of the pie, the best teachers for their kids, and the least amount of consequences for their child's mistakes. I'd better stop. It's not nice to meddle.

Kids sent into the future with this kind of an attitude don't stand a chance.

With a little tutoring, some kids develop mantra–like gratefulness as an extension of good manners. That's better than nothing. But it isn't necessarily authentic. Real gratefulness, true gratefulness, enjoys its finest moments when it originates from a genuinely thankful heart.

What kids desperately need is to be surrounded by love that spills over with unabashed appreciation. When we as parents decide to not only let God be our *God*, but let him be the Master of our lives as well, then this living testimony has the power to move gratefulness from a mantra to a mainstay in our children's makeup. When God is our master—and we realize that we've been bought and paid for at such a high price—thankfulness becomes a permanent part of our second nature. Our attitude doesn't reflect a nice little polite, "Thanks." Rather, it's a deep from the gut, straight through the heart THANK YOU!

You've heard the old saying, "What goes around comes around?" It's true; but it's especially true of gratefulness. For parents who really want to love their children, show them what true gratefulness looks like, and then watch them turn around and try it on you.

# 38

## Love That Encourages Candor

"Dad. Mom. We need to talk. I'm frustrated, hurt, and angry. And *guess what*? You're the reason." Do your kids have the freedom to approach you like that? Kids brought up in homes that encourage candor do.

Note the word: *Candor*. I could have said *honesty*. But I didn't . . . on purpose. That's because unbridled and unvarnished honesty can just about kill. That "sticks and stones" ditty we learned as children is a lie. Words not only do hurt; they can destroy relationships—sometimes for good. That's why loving our children requires that we offer truth that runs through a filter of grace. You end up with candor.

Candor isn't about catching people off guard to make them look worse than they are. It's not even close. Candor is ratcheted several steps above honesty. It's a way of communicating freely without prejudice or malice. It takes the truth and frames it in a way that helps rather than harms. There's also a high degree of *fairness* brought to bear within a home that operates with candor.

These are homes where what is on a child's mind can end up as dinner dialogue without fear of payback. Children are free to speak openly—albeit respectfully—without fear that they will have their heads handed back to them on a stick. That's because homes with candor create give–and–take between parents and children that promotes honesty dipped in honor. Grace makes the difference because it keeps honesty from getting ugly. It promotes the free exchange of heartfelt issues to a much higher level of forthrightness—a *careful* forthrightness that guards the dignity of others. Grace–based candor is a road trip through the truth that keeps people from destroying each other along the way.

It might be about friendships, dating lives, inadequacies, spiritual battles, or even problems with us. Real love isn't afraid of these kinds of discussions. It welcomes them. And in the process everyone enjoys an environment where grudges gain no voice and chips have a hard time finding a willing shoulder to rest on.

Adapted from *Grace-Based Parenting*

## 39

# Love That Guards Their Rest

Maintaining a healthy pace involves a whole lot more than making sure everyone gets a good night's sleep. It's not a bad start, but it's a limited solution because it assumes that rest is merely a physical thing. Not so. Children not only need rest for their bodies, but for their emotions and spirits as well. That's why a commitment to being a rested family is as much about the pace we set as it is the sleep we log each night.

Picture this: a family gets plenty of sleep each night and yet still functions with an overwhelming sense of restlessness. There's reason for this. They're *hurried*. Not *in* a hurry, mind you, but hurried.

Often, families couldn't relax if they tried. They're uncomfortable with quiet, seldom satisfied, struggle with shifting moral standards, worry a lot about things they can't control, and aren't happy unless they are winning at whichever of life's games they're currently playing.

Did I get you on that list? Don't take it personally. I got myself, too. The hurried lifestyle is a common Western problem in most homes. But just because it's pervasive doesn't mean we give up and let it steal our families' sense of rest.

There is hope when it comes to this conflict. We may not be able to find rest *from* the fast–paced culture that surrounds us, but we can find rest *in* it. Jesus summed up the solution when He said, *"Come to me, all of you who are weary and overwhelmed by your circumstances, and I will give you rest"* (Matthew 11:28).

The Lord's words have a timeless ring to them. They stretch through twenty–plus centuries and long to wash over our families. They reassure us that our quest for rest is reachable. But it has to start *inside* before it can move *outside*. Families that figure this out produce kids who play harder, work smarter, and sleep sweeter. It's the logical conclusion of God's solution for rest: He loves us, He made us with a purpose, and He guarantees us hope.

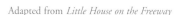

Adapted from *Little House on the Freeway*

50 Ways to Really Love Your Kids

# *Give Your Kids a Love That Fears God*

In the fear of the LORD there is strong confidence,
And His children will have a place of refuge.

PROVERBS 14:26 NKJV

His mercy is on those who fear Him
From generation to generation.

LUKE 1:50 NKJV

## 40

GIVE YOUR KIDS

# Love That Fears God

Most people assume that fear is a negative. As a result, they work overtime to avoid it. Actually, fear is quite an asset. It all depends on *what* we fear.

One fear puts all other fears in perspective. It validates the fears that protect us and overwhelms the ones that simply want to badger us.

It's the fear of God.

You knew I was going to say that. You looked at this chapter's title. What might have struck you as odd, however, is the fact that the title puts the words "love" and "fear" in the same statement as though they are interchangeable. When we're talking about a healthy fear of God, they are.

Some people within religious circles bristle at this concept. They prefer to avoid churches that suggest such a thing. If their pastor happens to slip and mention the possibility of fearing God in a sermon, these folks have flaming emails waiting for him by the time he gets home from Sunday lunch.

They assume that a God who is feared is automatically hard to love. It makes me wonder if they've ever met Him.

If they had, they'd not only welcome the concept of fearing Him, but they'd make it one of the major planks of their spiritual platforms. A healthy fear of God is simply recognizing the obvious and then embracing it in a practical way. God is the Creator; we're not. He holds the whole world in His hands; we can't. He knows the beginnings and the endings of our stories; we don't. He loves us with an everlasting love; we only wish.

Fearing God protects us and our children. This attitude says, "We recognize that although God's love is amazing, it is not to be abused. Although His standards are reasonable and loving, they are not to be ignored." There's one other tremendous benefit of fearing God. In a cathedral in London I saw an epitaph for a fellow named Lord Lawrence. This statement articulates a powerful advantage of fearing God:

*"He feared man so little, because he feared God so much."*

Put a little bit of that kind of fear into your children's hearts, and their lives will be a whole lot bolder.

# 41

## GIVE YOUR KIDS

# Love That Cultivates Courage

Like it or not, you and I are field commanders of a small but significant platoon of soldiers. Whether we appreciate the imagery is irrelevant. The battle is real. It's a war that rages against the moral security of our children's fragile spirits.

If they are going to stand a chance, we must train them. One of the main parts of our strategy should be instilling courage into their hearts. They need it now. They'll need it even more when they're out on their own.

Too many kids are having to face too much, too fast. The speed, complexity, and distortions of life try to drive a stake into the heart of our families as relationships run ragged, love gets litigated, truth becomes tentative, and opinion grows omnipotent.

Such a sophisticated challenge will require gut–deep resolve. That's why parents who really want to love their children must plant the seed of courage early and cultivate it every day.

When Howard Carter stuck his candle through a small hole in the ancient wall encasing King Tut's grave, his eyes were unprepared for the dazzling wealth that had lain in state for over three thousand years. Like any archaeologist, he assumed the gold, silver, and hundreds of furnishings were the real treasure. Yet there was another treasure, hardly detectable, but invaluable. In boxes and bowls near the sarcophagus of the young Pharaoh, Carter discovered grains of wheat that had been placed there to supply food for the king's trip through the nether world. No one figured those seeds, which had lay dormant for over three millennia, could ever sprout life.

But they did. Those seeds of wheat were planted, watered, and cultivated. And from those seeds came life. That wheat, which had sat in dark silence for so many centuries, proved to be the only thing alive in the whole tomb.

That's the nature of the right seed given the right conditions. Like the seed of courage. All it needs is a loving parent to plant it, cultivate it, and watch it grow.

Adapted from *Homegrown Heroes*

## 42

## GIVE YOUR KIDS

# Love That Brings the Best Out of Them

Wouldn't it be nice if we could distill the rhythm of life down to the crisp *left–right–left–right* cadence of a march? You'd know what's next every time. All you'd have to figure out is how to keep up.

Nice? Sure. Likely? No way.

If raising kids is anything, it's unpredictable. That's because it's not a march; it's a dance. The rhythms change all the time. Just when you think you've got the steps down, the tempo shifts into something you've never moved to before. It's not uncommon to feel like you're slam dancing in some endless family mosh pit most of the time.

Yet, in spite of all of this, we're still supposed to consistently bring the best out of them. I know something that helps. It's designed to counter the primary occupational hazard of parenting—exasperating our kids. Of all places, I found this advice in a drill sergeant's handbook.

But for it to work, it assumes that you are a careful student of your children and will commit to staying that way. Here's why: one of the things that brings the worst out of our children is when we fail to factor in the maturity and ability that they bring to any given challenge. This is where the good sergeant comes to the rescue.

If their maturity or ability is low, we need to *direct them*—tell them or show them what to do. If their maturity or ability is moderate, we need to *develop them*. How? Ask them questions like, "How do you think we should do this?" Or, "How have you done this in the past?" If their ability or maturity is high, we simply *delegate* the task and let them do it *their way*. You can see how exasperating it can be to a child if we delegate a task that he has either no ability or maturity to carry out. Conversely, instructing a child who is perfectly capable of carrying out a task is no fun either.

Here's the hint again: never stop studying your children. It's the surest way to love them by bringing the best out of them.

Adapted from *Basic Training for a Few Good Men*

# 43

# Love That Manages Its Fears

Fear is like a loaded gun. It's real handy if someone's trying to kill you, but dangerous if it's just lying around. Some people avoid fear at all cost, while others invest heavily in the sheer terror of it. Whether they're bungee jumping off a bridge or playing the stock market, fear fuels them, schools them, or fools them. And you can't predict how they'll respond. One person's thrill is another's paralysis—all because of this intangible force that haunts our souls and stalks us through our daily grinds.

God doesn't let us dance through life without forcing us to tango with fear occasionally. It's as much a part of our daily checklist as joy, confusion, contentment, or exhilaration. Some people understand fear better than others. We call them "courageous" people. They know that fear is the mettle within courage. They embrace it—making it their friend— so that it motivates them to do the right things at the right time, regardless of the cost.

Fear is one of the greatest gifts God has placed in the arsenal of human emotions. Fear of financial disaster kicks us out of bed in the morning and pushes us into the rat race.

Fear keeps us from getting into situations that are stacked against us. At the same time, fear gives us strength to prevail through those situations when they can't be avoided. Fear seizes us by the throat when the "mother of all temptations"—the kind that wrecks our marriages, our kids, and our reputations all at the same time—comes our way. If it were possible to calculate, we'd probably find that more families have been saved from moral ruin by raw fear than by their devotion to a moral code.

That's the good news. Here's the bad news. Fear is a four–letter word. It must be managed. Otherwise it can destroy the things you work for, defame the God you live for, and defraud the people for whom you'd be willing to die. Letting fear rule your family is not one of the seven deadly sins, but it ought to be. Do them a favor: love your kids enough to show them how to make fear their friend so it doesn't become their foe.

Adapted from *The High Cost of High Control*

## 44

GIVE YOUR KIDS

# Love That Never Gives Up on Them

*Road hats.* You may have never heard the term before, but you've seen them. These are ball caps that once were worn with pride. Now they're left to fade in the sun beside one of life's thoroughfares.

I feel sorry for them.

This probably isn't the smartest thing to mention in a book, but I've been known to go to their rescue. I know what you're thinking: "What kind of a low–life is Tim, anyway? Why would he want a hat that was on some stranger's head? Does he know where it's been? Has he no class?"

Let me answer the last question first. "No." I was born with a plastic spoon in my mouth. I believe that the best cologne a man can wear is sweat from a hard day's work. A blue–collar upbringing is hard to change. Besides, I don't really *wear* road hats; I just *rescue* them.

They remind me of something. Actually, they remind me of someone. Kids, in fact. Kids who get left behind in life for some reason.

Like the chubby kid being ridiculed at McDonald's because he's too wide to fit through the maze in the play area. Or the girl with the mousy face who stands against the wall at her high school homecoming but never gets asked to dance. How about the kid with the ear full of rings and the chip on his shoulder who has no one to help him wrestle with the dilemmas of life. There's the average kid on the fringe of the popular crowd, the slow and clumsy kid watching the game from the bench, the black kid in the white school, the poor kid in the upper–crust school, or the social misfit who eats lunch at school by himself.

All kids need someone to notice them, to reach out to them, to believe in them, and to never give up on them even after everyone else has. When they're hardest to love is when they need our love the most. They may be our culture's road hats— abandoned by the road of life. But all it takes to change that is for a parent to hit the brakes, back up, and rescue them.

Adapted from *"Road Hats"*

## 45

# Love That Is Known for its Generosity

Can you indulge me for a moment? I'd like to use the concept of tipping to make a bigger point about parenting.

Some folks enjoy standing close to generous people. Waiters, bellhops, valets, street people. What they all have in common is that their success—even survival—is dependent upon people giving them something they are not required to give. If it's coming their way, it's coming because someone decided to be *generous.* Obviously, all but one on that list are providing a service. Theirs is a minimum wage that they will be paid regardless of what others do. But for them to *thrive*, it's going to come down to how generously people choose to treat them.

Doesn't the level of generosity depend on the service they provide? Yes, if you prefer to live in a stark black and white world. But it doesn't matter in the world of grace. For those who live in grace, quality of service has little bearing on the choice to be generous.

That's because generous people aren't looking for an opportunity to be served; they are looking for an opportunity to bless.

It's easy to see how this principle affects our children. Our kindness can be tied to their performance—which is how the world around them allocates it. Or we can make generosity an unconditional byproduct of them simply being children . . . our children.

The Bible says God causes rain to fall on the good people as well as the not–so–good (Matthew 5:45). Why? Because everyone benefits from a soothing glass of water. God doesn't restrict His blessings to those who jump through all the right hoops. His blessings are simply a reflection of His generous heart. He blesses us because He loves us.

Obviously, there is nothing wrong with tying certain *privileges* and *freedoms* to the level of personal responsibility of an individual child. That's just smart parenting. But *generosity* is something completely different. It's a choice that springs from an attitude.

There's a difference—a huge difference—between blessing children and spoiling them, between giving them a hand–up or a hand–out. Parents whose hearts beat in sync with the heart of God find it easy to make the distinction.

## 46

GIVE YOUR KIDS

# Love That Is Honored to Serve Them

It was in literature class, about the tenth grade, when most of us were introduced to the poetic possibility that we were actually in charge of our lives. That's when students typically read William Earnest Henley's famous rhyme, "Invictus," which closes with that classic line, *I am the master of my fate; I am the captain of my soul.*

Actually, William. No, you're not.

You never were.

Nobody is.

Regardless of how nice it sounds in an epic poem, reality says that none of us really *own* our lives. The only free choice we actually exercise in life is the one where we decide whose servant we are going to be. We either choose to let God be the master of our life, or by default we put our lives at the mercy of the darker forces that want to claim our souls. After this, the natural consequence of our choice takes over.

Failure to understand this not only creates a gaping hole in our plans to prepare our children for adult success, but we actually set them up to be mastered by the very things that cause them to fail.

The key characteristic of people who have handed over their hearts to God is that they not only have a servant attitude toward others, but they see service as an *honor*. The fact that we can actually be living, breathing agents of God's love, emissaries of His amazing grace, moves service from a burden to a privilege. And the greatest opportunity we have to exercise this honor is in our homes.

Children who grow up in homes with parents who consider it an honor to care for them don't find ridicule or guilt waiting for them when the tasks get tough. Rather, they find a kind determination covered with sweat.

Just think! We get to be God's hands when our children's burden is too heavy, His eyes when they cannot find their way, His voice when they need an encouraging word, and His arms and lips when they desperately long for a tender touch.

Adapted from *Raising Kids for True Greatness*

# 47

## GIVE YOUR KIDS

# Love That Is Grateful to Sacrifice

Our Western inclination is to make life as pleasant as possible. How about three cheers for Western inclination: "Hip, hip, hooray!"

There's nothing wrong with wanting to make the burdens we carry as light as possible. I'm a great fan of disposable diapers for the little ones and DVDs in the SUVs for the bigger ones.

But we must be careful not to let our need for ease and comfort overwrite our God–given calling to sacrifice for our children. We have to be willing to give generously of our time, energy, money, sleep, and occasionally even our reputations for the best interests of our kids. Egos must be kept in check, pride has to be swallowed, and you'll probably have to stay up many nights until the last one is safely home. I figure it's the least we can do based on the sacrifice God made for us.

Being willing to sacrifice our lives for our children is the natural next step of a deep–seated love for God. The sheer power of our sacrifices cannot be quantified. Nor can they be minimized. When kids see just how unselfishly our faith lives itself out, they'll be far more inclined to want that kind of faith too.

When I was a child, a missionary visited my Sunday school class. She said, "A long time ago, before there was airline travel, missionaries would have to pack up their belongings and put them on steamer ships to get to their mission field. Often it would take months before they arrived. But what they packed their belongings *in* told the whole story about how much they were willing to sacrifice for what they were doing. They packed all of their earthly belongings in caskets. That's because most of the places they were going to were hostile to the gospel and there was a real chance that they could lose their lives. Regardless, most planned on staying there until they died." That kind of sacrifice is compelled by pure *love*.

Our kids need that kind of love. They'll know if we're willing to die for them by how grateful we are to *live* for them . . . especially at great sacrifice.

Adapted from *Why Christian Kids Rebel*

## 48

## GIVE YOUR KIDS

# Love That Looks Out for Them

We are an easily entertained society. I ought to know . . .

On Saturday mornings my siblings and I would get up to watch cartoons. It was long before 24–hour programming, Nickelodeon, and the Cartoon Network. Sometimes we'd park ourselves in front of the television before the stations came on the air for their morning lineup. We'd turn on the TV anyways, and a thing called a "screen test" would be staring back at us. It played a single tone—an E flat. (We found it on the piano.)

We'd watch it!

Sometimes we'd even harmonize to the tone. This shows just how easily we can be entertained. And lest you think I'm going to go into a diatribe against having a television in your house, relax. There are six televisions in our house. And I can give you three good reasons for them: NFL, NBA, and PGA. You can shove all those letters together to make the mother of all good reasons: ESPN.

Televisions aren't a threat to our families. How can they be? They all have On/Off switches and channel selectors. They only show us what we ask them to show us. Whether it's television in particular or entertainment in general, love constrains us as parents to run interference for our children and help them make good choices.

Love must filter life for our kids.

We'd never let some guy in a hazard suit walk through our front doors and pour toxic waste all over our kids. In the same way, we must be diligent to guard the hearts of our children from the noxious philosophies of our culture that want to enter their hearts through entertainment. Whether it's television, movies, music, websites, or video games, we need to be vigilant to look out for their best interests.

When they're young, we must *protect* their fragile emotions and vulnerable naiveté. But as they move into those teenaged years we need to shift our strategy into *preparing* them to make wise moral choices when it comes to entertainment.

It's how savvy parents produce savvy kids. Trust me, it's part of the winning formula of parents who want to really love their kids.

## 49

GIVE YOUR KIDS

# Love That Aims Them in the Right Direction

The line of parents who desire great success for their children could stretch around the world. I'm standing in it . . . right behind you. Who wouldn't want that? We love our children more than ourselves. We're surrendering the best years of our lives to give them as much of a head start towards an effective future as possible.

Here's the problem: it's hard not to take our cues from the culture that surrounds us. The question we should ask is, "Does our culture have a clue of what it is talking about?"

I don't think it does.

My conclusion comes from the targets where conventional wisdom suggests we aim our kids. There are about a dozen or so usual suspects in the lineup. I'll hit on the top four.

First comes the popular couple *health and beauty*. These aren't bad qualities to have in the future. The problem is when they're necessities in our formula for success. Health is unpredictable and beauty is superficial. They have absolutely no bearing on character. Another usual suspect is *power.* People scoff that the future won't be handed to the meek. They forget that Jesus promised the meek will inherit the earth (Matthew 5:5). Then, of course, there's *money and wealth.* This combination is probably the number one priority that parents whisper in their children's ears. Lastly there's *fame.*

Health and beauty, power, wealth, and fame. These four qualities are what most parents encourage their children to pursue. Oh, my dear friend, if you have pointed any of your kids in those directions as their primary goals, you've encouraged them to aim extremely *low.*

Jesus gave us a much better target to aim them towards. He said, "Love the LORD your God with all of your heart, with all of your soul, with all of your mind, and with all of your strength" and "love your neighbor as yourself" (Mark 12:30–31).

Love God passionately, love others enthusiastically. It's the lifestyle of the truly rich and famous. Kids who pursue this path *cannot fail.* You can make it easy for them to find the way. Just have them . . . follow you.

Adapted from *Raising Kids for True Greatness*

## 50

# Love That Does the Difficult Things

A young father struggling with his marriage said this to me: "I'm not into changing diapers. I'll play with the kid, read to him, keep an eye on him, but if he needs his diapers changed, count me out. I'm sorry, but *I don't do diapers.*" I could see why his marriage was in trouble.

Everybody has something they don't like to do. It might be cleaning house, folding clothes, driving car pool, waiting at practices, or going to church. So we don't clean it, fold it, drive it, wait at it, or go to it.

The problem slips even deeper. We're terrified of speaking in public, so we remain silent at a PTA meeting while a misguided parent drives some godless agenda down the throats of the school administration. We're afraid of rejection and reprisal so we remain mute while one of our children maintains a self–destructive habit. Or we're afraid of looking like a fool so we refuse to follow a clear leading of God in a particular matter with our kids.

Here's an observation I've made: the difference between the parents who achieve true greatness in their families is corollary to their willingness to do the things they don't want to do. It's like the marathon. The people who consistently finish are the ones who, during the months of training, laced on their shoes and took off before dawn in the cold and rain while the rest of the world was hitting the snooze button.

Jesus put it this way, "Whoever wants to become great among you must be your servant" (Matthew 20:26 NIV).

So we might not like to do windows, diapers, math homework, or bedtime stories. But real love can't afford to think, "What's in it for me." No, real love says "What's in it for them." It's the difference between parenting and *great* parenting.

I'm grateful that Moses didn't say, "I don't do Red Seas." David didn't say, "I don't do giants." Paul didn't say, "I don't do road trips." John didn't say, "I don't do Revelations." Mary didn't say, "I don't do virgin births." And I'm most grateful that Jesus didn't say, "I don't do crosses."

See what I mean?

Adapted from "I Don't Do Windows"

## 51

## Give Your Kids

# Love That Ultimately Lets Them Go

I remember the day I took the training wheels off my son's bike. It was a big day in his life. It was a huge day in mine. I straddled his bike behind him as we both stood atop a mild hill in the park. After whispering a few final instructions and words of encouragement in his ear, I planted a kiss on the top of his head . . . and he was off.

As my wife and I watched his blond hair bob in sync with each rut in the terrain, we knew we were watching a metaphor. Within this little scene in the park, a son was not only a student, but a teacher. Our hearts took careful notes.

He didn't ride far. Not that day. But he would, eventually. He had to. That's what he was made to do. He was never ours to keep; he was only ours to prepare for that day when his plans and purposes would take him over the hill and out of sight forever. It's a painful reality, but it has to happen. And this, too, is good.

For now, he was tethered to us. We could still reel him in for dinner. He was still close enough to call out for help in climbing down from a tree or for working out a solution to one of life's many riddles.

But the dependence that marked his early years eventually would yield to the independence of his growing up. As he pedaled farther from our lives we would have to make the courageous choice to let him go. He mastered the two–wheeler that day, but eventually he wanted to go back to four. Before very long, just like your kids, we knew he would be grabbing the car keys off the hook in the kitchen and racing out the door.

Our son mastered his first day without training wheels, just like he has mastered so many other lessons in growing up. As we walked back to the car I held his bike in my left hand and my wife's hand in my right. Her tight squeeze told me she had shared my thoughts. As we watched our son walking so confidently ahead of us, we knew it was just a matter of time before he'd be looking out from the front seat of his car and waving goodbye for good. That moment will come sooner than you think. That's because when it comes to raising our children the days are long . . . but the years are short.

Adapted from *Homegrown Heroes*

# Acknowledgements

Grateful acknowledgement is made to the following for permission to reprint material used in this book from the published works of Tim Kimmel:

*Basic Training for a Few Good Men* (Nashville: Thomas Nelson Publishers, 1997).

*Grace-Based Parenting* (Nashville: W Publishing Group, 2004).

*High Cost of High Control* (Scottsdale, Arizona: Family Matters, 2005).

*Homegrown Heroes* (Scottsdale, Arizona: Family Matters, 2005).

*Little House on the Freeway* (Sisters, Oregon: Multnomah Publishers, Inc., 1994).

*Raising Kids for True Greatness* (Nashville: W Publishing Group, 2006).

*Raising Kids Who Turn Out Right* (Scottsdale, Arizona: Family Matters, 2005).

*Why Christian Kids Rebel* (Nashville: W Publishing Group, 2004).

# About the Author

DR. TIM KIMMEL and his wife, Darcy, are the founders of Family Matters®. Committed to equipping families to appropriate the power of God's grace for every age and stage of life, Tim is one of America's top advocates speaking for the family today. He has sold more than 750,000 books and videos including *Grace–Based Parenting, Why Christian Kids Rebel,* his bestseller *Little House on the Freeway,* and *Raising Kids Who Turn Out Right.* Tim has hosted his own nationally syndicated radio program, speaks throughout the country, and enjoys life with his wife, his four children, their spouses, and his growing number of grandchildren.

For more information about
the Kimmels and Family Matters, please visit:
www.familymatters.net

*Grow in the grace and knowledge of
our Lord and Savior Jesus Christ.
Glory be to him now and forever! Amen.*

2 Peter 3:18 ncv